Fun and Easy
Drawing

Fun and Easy Drawing
Storybook Characters

Rosa M. Curto

Enslow Elementary

an imprint of

Enslow Publishers, Inc.

40 Industrial Road
Box 398
Berkeley Heights, NJ 07922
USA

http://www.enslow.com

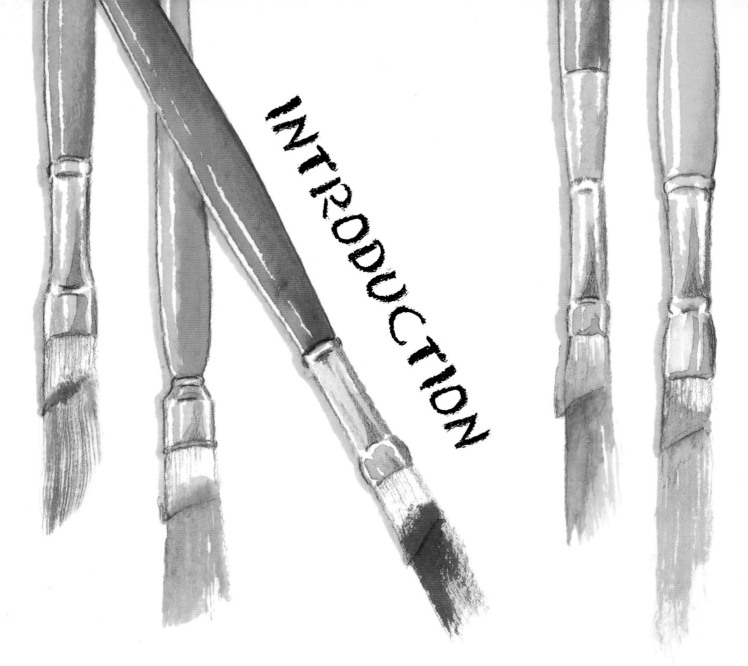

INTRODUCTION

Making art is a fun way to express yourself. You can create your own world and the characters that live in it! There are many different tools you can use to make art, such as markers, colored pencils, crayons, and paint. It would be best to draw in pencil first so if you make a mistake, you can erase it and try it again. Then, once you are happy with your drawing, you can color it in any way you wish.

SOME TIPS BEFORE YOU START DRAWING:

- CHOOSE A QUIET AND WELL-LIT PLACE TO WORK.

- HAVE WHAT YOU NEED TO DRAW AT HAND.

- TAKE YOUR TIME.

- HAVE FUN!

JESTER

Start with three simple shapes:
a circle, a square, and a trapezoid.
Add the arms and the legs.

1

Draw the shirt collar.
Start the hat.

2

Finish drawing the
hat and collar.

3

4

Finish the arms and legs. Draw the hands and feet.

5

Draw a smiling face.

6

Finish the details. Color him in as you wish!

A JESTER WEARS BRIGHT AND COLORFUL CLOTHING. HIS JOB IS TO ENTERTAIN THE ROYAL COURT.

BALLERINA

Look at the head and body: they are very simple shapes. Draw the arms and legs.

1

Finish the body and erase the lines.

2

LOOK!
After you erase the lines, you have the dress.

3

Draw the hair and face.

Finish the arms and legs.
Draw the shoes.

Finish the details
and color her in.

6

SHE DANCES TO
BEAUTIFUL MUSIC.

SULTAN

Start with a circle and a rectangle.
Draw the arms, hands, and legs.

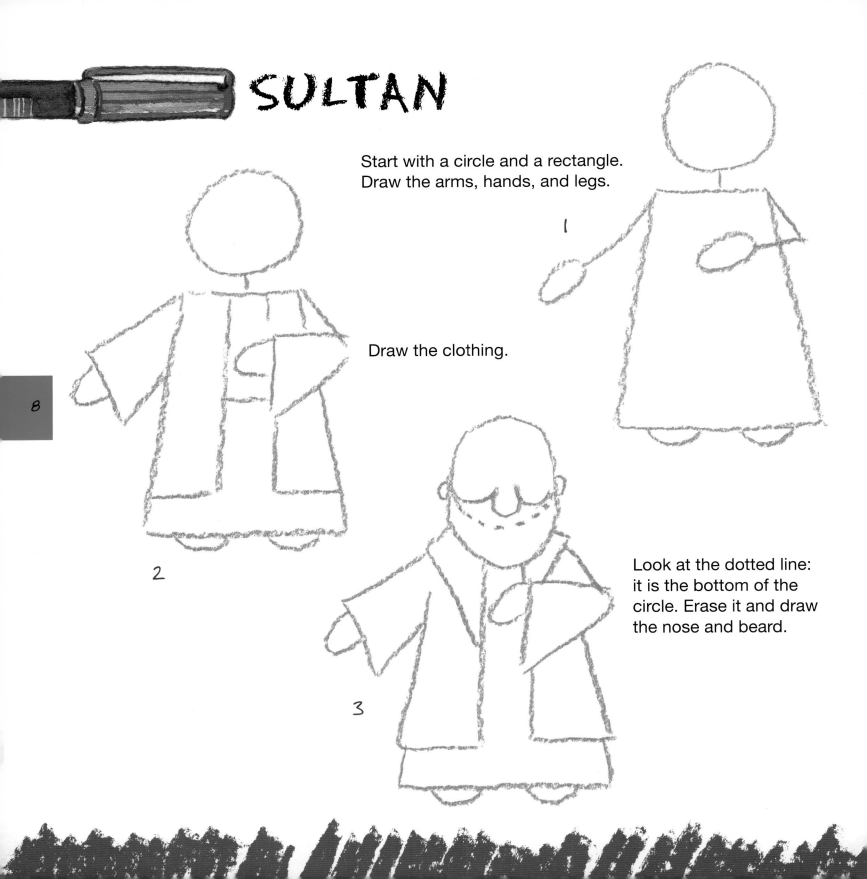

1

Draw the clothing.

2

Look at the dotted line:
it is the bottom of the
circle. Erase it and draw
the nose and beard.

3

Draw a hat, eyes, and hands. Give him a royal staff.

4

Finish the details and color him in.

5

A SULTAN RULES A KINGDOM.

AMERICAN INDIAN

Draw the head and body with simple shapes.

Draw a basket under her arm.

Draw the arms, hands, and face. Add a headband and shoes.

1

2

3

4

Draw two long ponytails and a couple of feathers.

Finish the details.

5

Color her in.

6

SHE RESPECTS MOTHER EARTH. SHE THANKS NATURE FOR GIVING PEOPLE WATER, ANIMALS, AND PLANTS.

CHIEF OF THE TRIBE

Draw these four shapes.

Add an arm
and a leg.

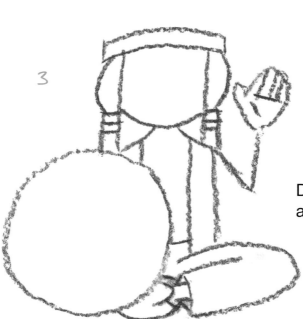

Draw the hair, hand,
and waist.

Finish the arm and
add two feathers.

Draw the rest of
the headdress.

13

Finish the details and color him in.

THE CHIEF LEADS HIS PEOPLE.

MAGICIAN

Draw two simple shapes for the head and body. Add the arms and legs.

1

Draw the front of the jacket.

2

3

Draw the collar, bow tie, sleeves, and belt.

4

Finish the hands.
Draw a hat on his head.

5

Finish the details
and color him in.

6

15

THE MAGICIAN CAN MAKE STARS AND
COLORED SCARVES COME OUT OF HIS
MAGIC WAND. HE CAN ALSO PULL A
BUNCH OF FLOWERS, DOVES, AND EVEN
A RABBIT OUT OF HIS HAT.

CLOWN 1

1

Draw a circle, square, and rectangle.

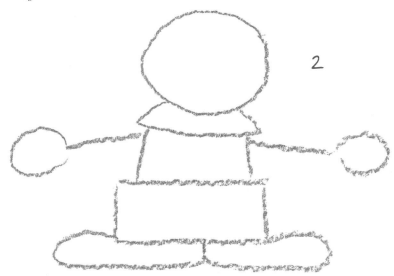

2

Draw the collar, arms, hands, and feet.

Draw her pants
with suspenders.

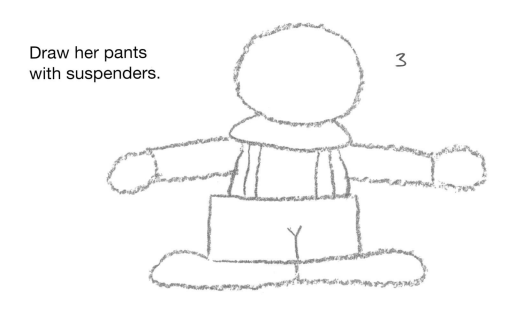

3

Draw a smiling face.

4

Draw a hat with flowers
and two pigtails.

5

Finish the details and color her in.

SOME CLOWNS ENTERTAIN
AT THE CIRCUS. THEY MAKE
PEOPLE LAUGH.

6

CLOWN 2

Draw a circle and a square.
Add the legs and arms.

1

Draw the hat and the collar.

2

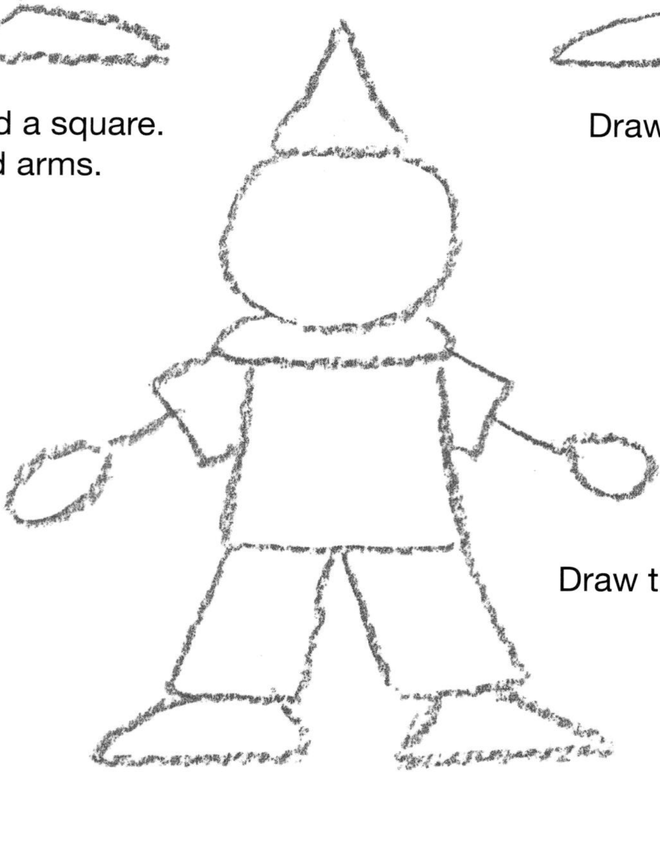

Draw the shirt and pants.

3

4 Give him some hair.
Finish the arms and add a watch.

Draw the face and a guitar.

5

19

6 Finish the details and color him in.

SOME CLOWNS MAKE PEOPLE LAUGH
BY WEARING FUNNY COSTUMES.

PIRATE

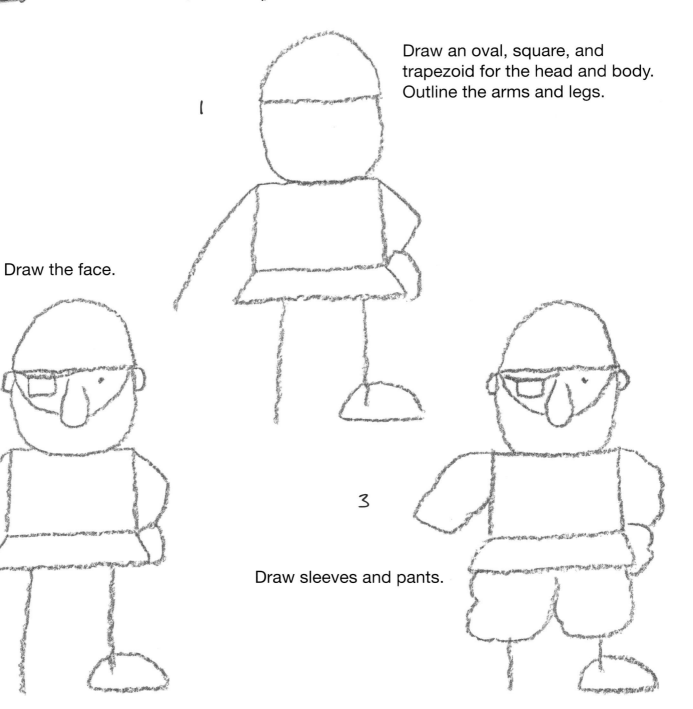

1 Draw an oval, square, and trapezoid for the head and body. Outline the arms and legs.

Draw the face.

2

3

Draw sleeves and pants.

Finish the hat. You can give him a hook and a wooden leg if you wish.

4

5

Finish the details and color him in.

PIRATES SAIL THE SEAS LOOKING FOR TREASURE.

6

PRINCE

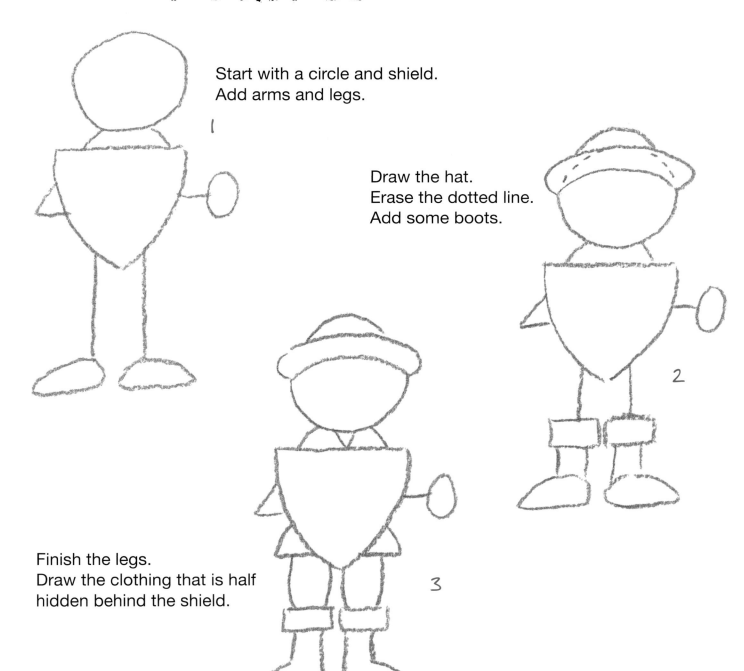

Start with a circle and shield.
Add arms and legs.

1

Draw the hat.
Erase the dotted line.
Add some boots.

2

Finish the legs.
Draw the clothing that is half
hidden behind the shield.

3

4

Draw a lance in his hand.

5

Give him a cape.

A PRINCE IS THE SON OF A KING AND QUEEN. IN STORYBOOKS, PRINCES ARE VERY BRAVE. THEY MAY EVEN FIGHT DRAGONS.

Finish the details and color him in.

6

PRINCESS

Draw an oval and a trapezoid.
Add the arms.

1

Outline the waist and
draw the hair.

2

Finish the dress.
Draw the neck and sleeves.

3

Add a bow and shoes.

4

Draw the hat,
belt, and scarf.

5

6

Color her in.

A PRINCESS IS THE
DAUGHTER OF A KING
AND QUEEN. IN STORIES,
SHE USES HER WITS TO
SAVE THE DAY.

KING

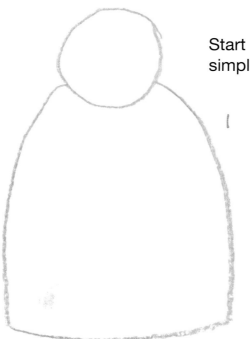

Start with two simple shapes.

1

Draw the nose, ears, beard, and collar.

2

Add details to the clothing. Draw the sleeves and hands.

3

4

Give him a crown and finish the hands.

Draw his face and give him a royal staff.

5

A KING IS A MAN WHO RULES A KINGDOM. HE LIVES IN A PALACE OR A CASTLE.

6

QUEEN

Start with two simple shapes.

1

Draw the cape
and the crown.

2

3

Draw the sleeves and the hands.

4

Finish the crown and the hands. Draw the collar.

5

Give her hair and a belt.

6

Finish the details and color her in.

A QUEEN IS A WOMAN WHO RULES A KINGDOM. SHE CAN RULE ALONE OR WITH A KING.

DANCER

Draw a circle and other simple shapes to make her head and body. Add the arms and legs.

Draw the sleeves.

Give her two scarves, one on the head and the other around the waist. Finish the feet.

4

Draw the hands.

Give her hair, earrings,
and bracelets.

5

SHE PLAYS THE
TAMBOURINE AS
SHE DANCES.

6

Draw her face and a
tambourine in her hands.

Color her in.

THE LANGUAGE OF ART

Look at these two boys, A and B.

Boy A falls over.

Boy B falls over and he is dizzy. His head is spinning.

Look at these two men, A and B.

Man A takes his hat off.

Man B takes his hat off and waves.

YOU CAN SHOW ACTIONS WITH LINES.

NOW LOOK!
On the left, there are two kinds of bubbles. Some can be filled with letters and others with symbols. These bubbles show what a character is saying or thinking.

AN EXCLAMATION POINT CAN SHOW A CHARACTER IS SURPRISED.

A QUESTION MARK CAN SHOW A CHARACTER DOES NOT KNOW SOMETHING.

"POOF" IS JUST ONE NOISE YOU CAN SPELL OUT.

A LIGHTBULB OR A CANDLE CAN SHOW THAT A CHARACTER HAD A BRIGHT IDEA.

A BUNCH OF LETTER ZS MEANS A CHARACTER IS SLEEPING.

FOOD MEANS A CHARACTER IS THINKING ABOUT EATING.

RAIN CLOUDS CAN SHOW THAT A CHARACTER IS IN A BAD MOOD.

MUSIC NOTES CAN MEAN A CHARACTER IS WHISTLING.

HEARTS CAN MEAN A CHARACTER IS IN LOVE.

Here are some symbols without bubbles.

MUSIC NOTES WITH A SQUIGGLY LINE CAN MEAN A CHARACTER IS LISTENING TO MUSIC.

YOUR CHARACTER SEES STARS WHEN HE OR SHE GETS HIT IN THE HEAD OR FALLS OVER.

Different ways of running:

STAGGERING, JUMPING   JOGGING   RUNNING REALLY FAST

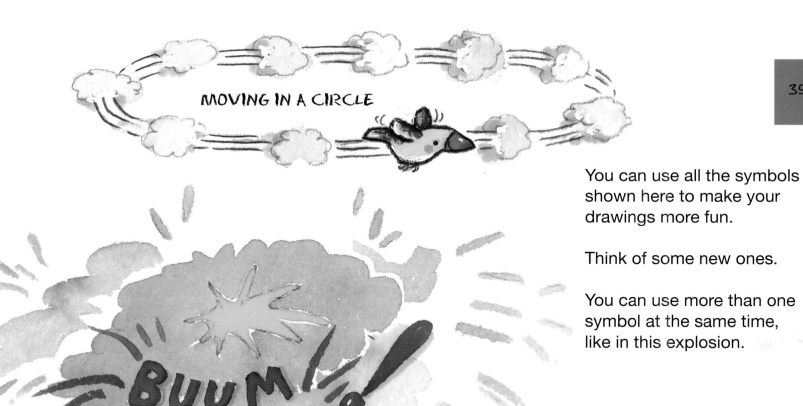

MOVING IN A CIRCLE

You can use all the symbols shown here to make your drawings more fun.

Think of some new ones.

You can use more than one symbol at the same time, like in this explosion.

BUUM!

HAVE FUN DRAWING!

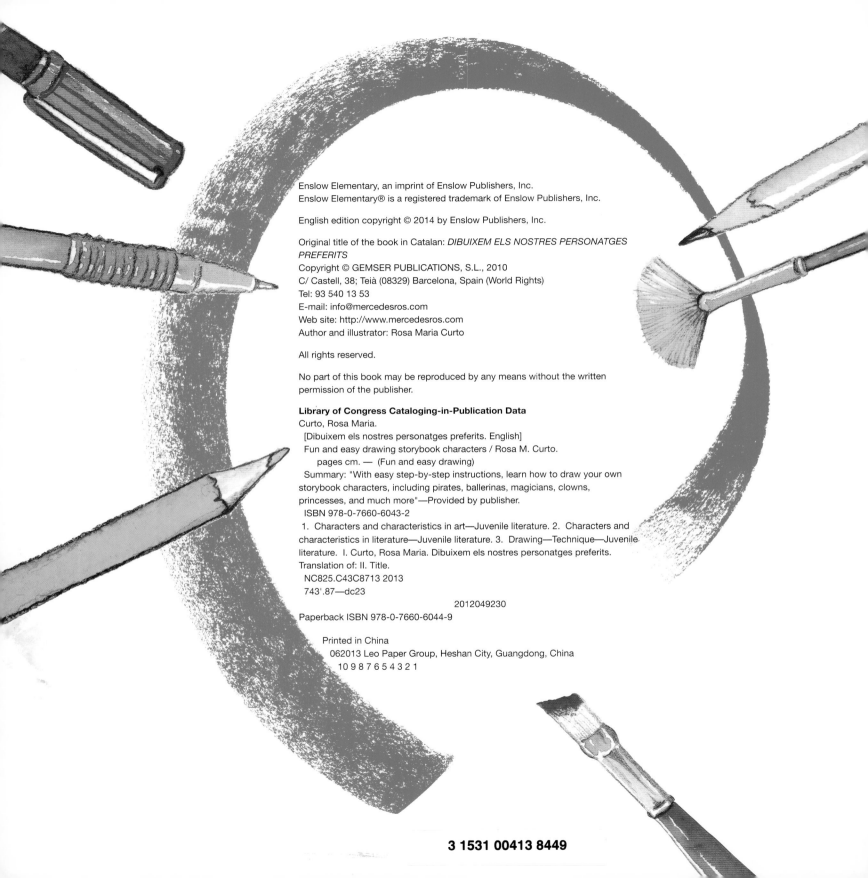

Enslow Elementary, an imprint of Enslow Publishers, Inc.
Enslow Elementary® is a registered trademark of Enslow Publishers, Inc.

English edition copyright © 2014 by Enslow Publishers, Inc.

Original title of the book in Catalan: *DIBUIXEM ELS NOSTRES PERSONATGES PREFERITS*
Copyright © GEMSER PUBLICATIONS, S.L., 2010
C/ Castell, 38; Teià (08329) Barcelona, Spain (World Rights)
Tel: 93 540 13 53
E-mail: info@mercedesros.com
Web site: http://www.mercedesros.com
Author and illustrator: Rosa Maria Curto

Library of Congress Cataloging-in-Publication Data
Curto, Rosa Maria.
  [Dibuixem els nostres personatges preferits. English]
  Fun and easy drawing storybook characters / Rosa M. Curto.
      pages cm. — (Fun and easy drawing)
  Summary: "With easy step-by-step instructions, learn how to draw your own storybook characters, including pirates, ballerinas, magicians, clowns, princesses, and much more"—Provided by publisher.
  ISBN 978-0-7660-6043-2
  1. Characters and characteristics in art—Juvenile literature. 2. Characters and characteristics in literature—Juvenile literature. 3. Drawing—Technique—Juvenile literature. I. Curto, Rosa Maria. Dibuixem els nostres personatges preferits. Translation of: II. Title.
  NC825.C43C8713 2013
  743'.87—dc23
                                    2012049230
Paperback ISBN 978-0-7660-6044-9

  Printed in China
    062013 Leo Paper Group, Heshan City, Guangdong, China
    10 9 8 7 6 5 4 3 2 1